Colours

Activities for 3–5 Year Olds

Irene Yates

Brilliant
PUBLICATIONS

We hope you enjoy using this book. If you would like further information on other titles published by Brilliant Publications, please write to the address given below or look on our website: www.brilliantpublications.co.uk.

Other books in the Activities for 3–5 Year Olds series:

All About Us

Caring and Sharing

Families

Food

Gardening

Pets

Shopping

Water

Weather

Published by Brilliant Publications,
Unit 10, Sparrow Hall Farm, Edlesborough, Bedfordshire, LU6 2ES
website: www.brilliantpublications.co.uk

Written by Irene Yates
Second edition revised and updated in 2012 by Debbie Chalmers
Illustrated by Claire Boyce

© Irene Yates
Printed ISBN 978 0 85747 661 6
ebook ISBN 978 0 85747 078 2

The Publisher accepts no responsibility for accidents arising from the activities described in this book.

First published in 1998, 2008, second edition 2012
10 9 8 7 6 5 4 3 2 1

Contents

To avoid the clumsy 'he/she', the child is referred to throughout as 'she'.

Introduction

Recognizing, identifying and being able to name colours is an essential step in the early education of all children. Knowing colours and having some idea of the concept of colour gives them a means of making comparisons and a way of observing and exploring their immediate environment.

The activities are linked to the Early Learning Goals of the Department for Education's revised *Statutory Framework for the Early Years Foundation Stage* (September 2012), and its guidance document, *Development Matters*. They respect the children's developing skills, abilities and self-images and encourage them to form positive relationships with each other and with the adults in their setting, as well as with their families at home.

Children learn through playing and exploring, creating and thinking critically. The role of an early years practitioner is to provide stimulating and challenging activities within an enabling environment. Ideas must be flexible enough to meet the needs of each individual as a unique child and to build upon the children's knowledge and interests to promote active learning. All of the activities in this book may be easily adapted to suit individual children or groups of any size.

Look out for children, particularly boys, who have real difficulty in discerning certain colours, as they may be displaying symptoms of colour-blindness.

These children will need some specialist help, support and understanding while they find other ways of accessing activities that rely heavily on colours.

The book uses materials which are likely to be readily available within your class or group's location, or which can be easily provided by the children's families or carers, if requested.

All of the activities are designed to give the children confidence and feelings of achievement which, in turn, will become effective tools for learning.

Sorting colours

Learning opportunities
* Developing understanding and speaking skills within a familiar group
* Matching colours, learning and remembering their names
* Beginning to distinguish between and read colour names

Links to the Early Learning Goals
* Communication and language – Understanding, Speaking

Also
* Literacy – Reading

Equipment and resources
Lots of different coloured objects, different coloured sheets of sugar paper, felt-tipped pen, small pieces of card for name labels.

Activity
Invite a small group of children to work together to sort the objects into sets of different colours. Talk about the colours, saying their names frequently and encouraging the children to repeat the words. Ask the children to sort all the blue things, all the red things and all the yellow things (and any other colours you have) into groups and to place them on the appropriate sheets of coloured sugar paper.

Extension

Write the colour names carefully on pieces of card. Put each colour name card with the appropriate coloured objects. Point out the word clearly, running your finger along it slowly in the left to right direction.

Discussion

Invite the children to count how many red things or yellow things they have, or to decide which group has the most or the least items. Encourage them to try to read the words and to put each word on the right coloured paper.

Can you bring it?

Learning opportunities
* Developing listening, concentration and imaginative thinking skills
* Responding and adding to a group discussion
* Speaking confidently within a familiar group

Links to the Early Learning Goals
* Communication and language – Listening and attention, Understanding, Speaking

Also
* Expressive arts and design – Being imaginative

Equipment and resources
Space to sit together.

Activity
Invite a group of children to sit with you to play a game called 'Colour party'. Someone chooses a colour and begins the game by saying, for example, 'I'm having a colour party and I've got a yellow banana.' Everyone else listens carefully to hear what colour has been chosen and thinks of something appropriate that they could bring. For example, the next player could say, 'I'm bringing a yellow lemon.' The game continues until the children can't think of any more things of that colour, then someone else is chosen to begin again with a new colour.

Extension
Play 'I went shopping' and get everyone to preface what they buy with a colour.

Discussion

Talk about the number of different colours there are and challenge adults and children to think of as many as they can. If you include different shades and less well-known names, you could create a very long list! Older children may be interested to look at boxes of artists' pencils or watercolour paintboxes for more ideas, or to listen to the song from 'Joseph And The Amazing Technicolor Dreamcoat'. Ask children if they can think of ten things that are naturally a colour such as red, blue, yellow or green – not toys which have been painted or made from coloured plastic.

Steps

Learning opportunities

* Listening and responding to simple instructions, involving carrying out several ideas or actions simultaneously
* Developing control and coordination in whole body movements

Links to the Early Learning Goals

* Communication and language – Understanding

Also

* Physical development – Moving and handling

Equipment and resources

A large floor space indoors or level ground area outdoors; at least eight large circles in four different colours; sticky tape (double-sided if possible).

Activity

Stick the circles down on the floor or ground, about 20 cms apart, in a random pattern. The children take turns to move across the 'steps'. Give instructions such as 'Put one foot on a red circle. Put the other foot on a green circle. Put one hand on a red circle. Put the other hand on a blue circle.' Encourage the children to move their hands and feet to the different circles, following the instructions.

Extension

You can make this game more complex by adding squares to the circles and giving the children further to travel and more moves to choose from.

Discussion

Challenge the children to balance in different ways, such as on one leg, or on one hand and one leg, and to describe what they are doing.

Dancing bears

Learning opportunities
* Improving control of creative whole body movements
* Negotiating and sharing space safely
* Responding to music, following instructions and working confidently as a member of a group

Links to the Early Learning Goals
* Physical development – Moving and handling
Also
* Expressive arts and design – Being imaginative
* Personal, social and emotional development – Managing feelings and behaviour, Making relationships

Equipment and resources
A large space, indoors or outdoors, that is safe for movement activities; a source of music.

Activity
Encourage children to dance to the music and stop when the music stops. Each time it stops, an adult may give an instruction, such as 'Every bear who's wearing red shoes should sit down,' or 'Every bear whose name begins with the same sound as pink should sit down.' Children continue to dance, each time the music plays, gradually sitting down one by one, following the instructions given. The game ends when all the dancing bears are sitting down. Invite children to take turns to be the leader who gives instructions.

Extension

Instead of dancing randomly to the music, have the children following a leader, doing specific actions, like jumping or hopping.

Discussion

Discuss all the different colours the children are wearing. Discuss what sounds the colour names begin with. Offer ideas that the children may use in instructions when it is their turn to be the leader.

Traffic colours

Learning opportunities

* Improving control and coordination in large and small movements
* Negotiating and sharing space safely
* Following instructions in order to participate within a group
* Understanding the importance of physical exercise as a part of keeping healthy
* Developing an awareness of how to stay safe out in the local environment

Links to the Early Learning Goals

* Physical development – Moving and handling, Health and self-care

Also

* Communication and language – Understanding
* Understanding the world – The world

Equipment and resources

Three card circles in different colours – one red, one orange and one green; a large, safe space, either indoors or outdoors.

Activity

Gather the children together and invite them to sit as a group to play a game. Explain carefully that 'green is for go, orange (or amber) is for get ready and red is for stop'. Choose and demonstrate a movement, such as hopping in a straight line, jumping in all directions or walking on all fours in a circle, for the children to copy.

Hold up the red card for them to be still. Hold up the orange card at the same time, to get ready, then green on its own for go. Remind them to watch for the orange card and then the red card, to be ready and then stop. When they've stopped, change the movement.

Extension

Work with the children on different kinds of movement at different levels, such as walking on tiptoes, stretching, bending and crawling. Ask them to move in different directions.

Discussion

Talk with the children about how car drivers know when to stop at traffic lights and how the people know when it's safe to cross the road. Talk with the children about road safety precautions.

Red means hop

Learning opportunities

* Improving control and coordination in large and small movements
* Negotiating and sharing space safely
* Following instructions and responding appropriately in order to participate within a group

Links to the Early Learning Goals

* Physical development – Moving and handling

Also

* Communication and language – Listening and attention, Understanding
* Personal, social and emotional development – Managing feelings and behaviour

Equipment and resources

Three or more large card circles or squares in different colours; a large, safe space, either indoors or outdoors.

Activity

Show the children the different coloured cards and tell them that each colour is a clue to a certain movement. For example, red could mean hop, blue could mean jump, yellow could mean wobble like a jelly and green could mean clap your hands. Practise each movement separately with the children, until they are confident of what to do each time they see a colour.

Invite children to take turns to choose a card and hold it up, while the others respond with the correct movement.

Extension

Try using two cards at the same time and asking the children to make both of the movements, such as jumping and wobbling at the same time. Ask them to try performing the red, then yellow, then blue movements in quick succession.

Discussion

Invite the children to think up some more movements of their own and to describe them to the group before demonstrating them.

Two-coloured windmills

Learning opportunities
* Developing and improving control and coordination in large and small movements
* Exploring craft techniques, colour mixing and creative designs

Links to the Early Learning Goals
* Physical development – Moving and handling
Also
* Expressive arts and design – Exploring and using media and materials, Being imaginative

Equipment and resources
Shiny or gummed coloured paper, or white paper and coloured pens, pencils or crayons; sticks or straws; paper fasteners; hair pins; beads; scissors; rulers.

Activity
Work with two or three children at a time, to allow enough help and attention for each individual. Support the children as they measure out 20 cm squares of paper and cut them out. They will need to make two squares each, in different colours. They may either choose two different coloured papers or colour in two white squares. Stick the two squares of different colours together, back to back. Measure and draw two diagonal lines, from corner to corner.

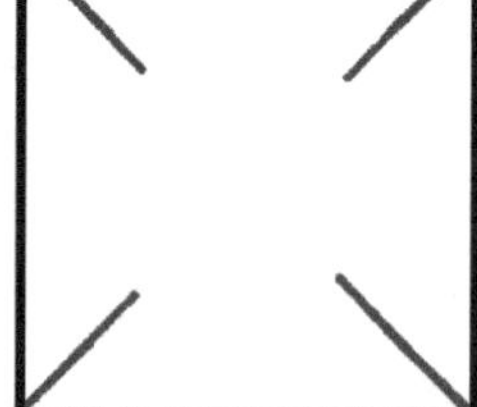

Cut along the lines, leaving 3 cm clear in the centre. Turn the left hand corner of each flap into the centre.

Push a hair pin through the front to secure the shapes, thread a bead onto the pin and then push it back into the stick, making sure that it doesn't protrude out of the back of the stick.

Extension

Blow the windmills to create a panorama of colour spinning round. Display them on the wall or in a huge pot, bound together with sticky tape, to keep them safe.

Discussion

Name the parts of the windmill and the techniques you are using as you work, mentioning the corners, the middle, sticking 'back to back' and folding corners down into the middle. Talk to the children about their choices of colours and what happens to the colours when you blow on the windmill and make it turn.

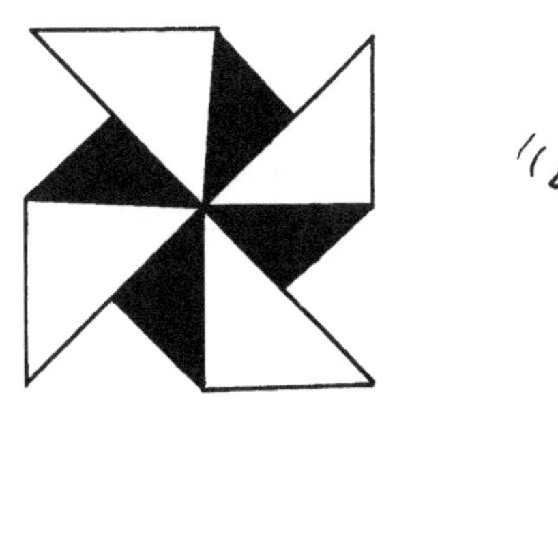

Colour sharing

Learning opportunities
* Working as a group, sharing and taking turns
* Cooperating to decide the order of turns and to help and support each other during a game
* Reinforcing the concepts of different colours and ordinal numbers

Links to the Early Learning Goals
* Personal, social and emotional development – Self-confidence and self-awareness, Making relationships

Also
* Communication and language – Understanding
* Mathematics – Numbers

Equipment and resources
No special equipment.

Activity
Invite a small group of children, who are learning about colours, to play a game. Decide who will go first and ask that child to look around the room and fetch for the group something that is yellow. Ask the other children to check her choice and decide who will be second. That child should then fetch a different yellow object and bring it to the other children, who will check its colour and choose who will be third. When all of the children have had one turn, begin a new round with a different colour and ask the children to decide on an altered order of players.

Extension

Make the game more challenging by asking the
children to bring 'something that is not red' or
'something that is not red and not green'. Encourage
them to name the colours of the objects they bring.

Discussion

Encourage children to notice who is wearing
something red or blue or green. Ask them to spot a
red brick or a green brick within a pile of construction
pieces or built into a model.

What colour would you like?

Learning opportunities
* Making positive relationships by displaying
  sensitivity to the needs and opinions of others
* Developing an awareness and an understanding
  that people have different needs and preferences
  and may make differing choices
* Understanding how to collect data from people in
  order to carry out research and make comparisons

Links to the Early Learning Goals
* Personal, social and emotional development –
  Making relationships

Also
* Understanding the world – People and
  communities
* Mathematics – Shape, space and measures

Equipment and resources
Paper, coloured crayons or felt-tipped pens.

Activity
Work with three or four children at a time. Each needs
a sheet of paper divided into eight sections. Invite
each child to write her name in one of the sections
and to colour a patch of it in her favourite colour.
Encourage them to go to adults and children within
the group and ask which are their favourite colours.
They may then write in other names and colour in the
sections appropriately. Support the children in writing
'Mummy' and 'Daddy', or the names of other people
that they live with, in the remaining sections. Suggest

that they ask parents or carers to fill in their sections,
either when they come to collect the children at the
end of a session, or at home.

Extension
Make a coloured bar chart showing how many people
like each colour best.

Discussion
Ask children to consider colours and to say which
they think are bright colours, strong colours, or
cheerful colours. Ask what blue or brown makes them
think about. Encourage them to say which colour
makes them feel happiest.

Colour display

Learning opportunities
* Selecting objects and materials independently for a chosen theme
* Sharing ideas and resources with others and taking an interest in their opinions and contributions
* Treating possessions and artefacts with care and respect

Links to the Early Learning Goals
* Personal, social and emotional development – Self-confidence and self-awareness, Managing feelings and behaviour, Making relationships

Also
* Understanding the world – People and communities

Equipment and resources
Tables, boxes or climbing blocks against a wall, on which to set up a display; smaller boxes of different sizes and heights; an appropriately coloured cloth or piece of fabric; felt-tipped pens; card.

Activity
Suggest to the children that you could make a colour display and discuss colours with the group until you all agree on a favourite colour to begin with. Arrange the small boxes on a table (or large box) so that you have an interesting display area. Cover it with an appropriate coloured cloth and put up a label saying, for example, 'Red things'. Ask the children to look for things for the display in the room and to

ring in things from home (Make sure things bought
rom home are clearly labelled with the child's name.)
Display the objects with the children's help. Talk about
each child's object with the group, then invite the child
o add it, carefully, to the display.

Extension

Encourage children to make appropriately coloured
paintings, drawings, collages and models to display on
the wall and the table.

Discussion

With the children, name all the objects in the display.
Talk about different shades of colour, using the words
'lighter than', 'darker than', 'lightest' , 'darkest', 'dull',
'bright'.

Blue Giant, Blue Giant

Learning opportunities

* Exploring a familiar story in order to create a similar one
* Reading, writing and drawing skills
* Developing imagination and sharing ideas within a group

Links to the Early Learning Goals

* Literacy – Reading, Writing

Also

* Communication and language – Listening and attention
* Expressive arts and design – Being imaginative

Equipment and resources

A copy of *Brown Bear, Brown Bear, What Do You See* by Bill Martin Jr; large sheets of card, stapled together to make a book; white and coloured paper; crayons, pens and pencils; scissors; glue.

Activity

Read the story to the children several times over a week or two, until they are very familiar with it and can recite the words along with you and describe all the pictures. Suggest that the group could make another story just like it, using 'Blue Giant' in place of 'Brown Bear'. Discuss ideas with the children, to decide what happens and what the Blue Giant sees. Plan the various pages and the order of the story together, then ask children to write their ideas into the book, supporting them or acting as a scribe when necessary. Encourage them to draw pictures to illustrate the story and to cut them out and stick them onto the appropriate pages, reading the words to find out where they should go.

Extension
Read the children's own book to them and keep it accessible so that they can choose to read it and share it together.

Discussion
Ask the children whether they want their story to be sensible or to have some silly pages on which crazy things happen. Encourage them all to join in with group discussions on, 'What could the Blue Giant see that's orange/green/pink/purple?' or 'Who can think of a good idea for a place that the giant could go to?' Hold up the book and invite children to read the words and remind the group what the page says.

My colour book

Learning opportunities
* Matching, sorting and identifying different colours
* Reading, writing and drawing skills

Links to the Early Learning Goals
* Literacy – Reading, Writing

Also

* Expressive arts and design – Exploring and using
  media and materials

Equipment and resources
Sheets of paper or card; stickers and gummed shapes
(in coloured paper, shiny paper, foam and felt);
scissors; felt-tipped pens, pencils and crayons; hole
punch; thread, string or wool.

Activity
Working with a small group, give each child six sheets
of paper or card and invite them to make their own
colour book. Each sheet will be a page and focus on
one colour. Children may use one side or both sides
of each, to make a six-page or twelve-page book.
Offer a free choice of the stickers and gummed shapes
and encourage children to place them on their pages,
grouping the colours together. They could try to make
their own pictures or just imaginative patterns and
designs. Give each child another sheet and invite her
to make a title page for her book, writing her chosen
title and her own name, with support if necessary.
Use the hole punch on all of the pages and tie them
together using thread, string or wool.

Extension

Ask the children to add words to each page. They can
be as simple as, 'This is my red page', etc. Encourage
children to write the words for themselves, but
allow them to trace or copy the writing or to make
their own marks and then dictate to a scribe where
necessary. Read the words with the children once they
are written, following them with a finger, from left to
right.

Discussion

Offer encouragement and support to children by
talking about their books as they make them. For
example, ask what they would like to put on the red/
blue/green page, what shapes they need to make their
picture or pattern, what they will choose to put on the
cover and what they will decide to call their book.

Colour count

Learning opportunities
* Developing and practising counting skills
* Understanding counting in ones (1–10) and in tens (10–100)

Links to the Early Learning Goals
* Mathematics – Numbers

Equipment and resources
Threading beads and strings (up to 10 strings and 100 beads if possible).

Activity
Work with individual children, pairs or small groups. Encourage children to choose a colour, count out 10 beads of that colour and thread them onto a string, to make a 'snake'. Stop after threading 10 beads and choose a different colour to thread onto a different string. Stop again when you have threaded 10 beads of that colour. Continue to make 'snakes' until all the beads are used, then lie the 'snakes' beside each other and count the beads on each one to check that they all have exactly 10.

Extension
Count all the beads on the snakes together, beginning at 1 and counting on to 11 and to 21, etc. Emphasize the numbers 10, 20, 30, etc, as you reach the last bead on each string. Try counting them in 10s, pointing to each snake in turn and saying only 10, 20, 30, etc. Then count how many snakes there are and talk about

the links between the numbers (4 snakes, with 10 beads each, have 40 beads; 6 snakes, with 10 beads each, have 60 beads).

Discussion

Which colour snake do you like the best? Can we make a multi-coloured snake with ten beads? Can we make a snake with a colour pattern?

Hide the ladybirds

Learning opportunities
* Counting skills
* Simple addition and subtraction
* Developing an awareness of multiplication through repeated addition

Links to the Early Learning Goals
* Mathematics – Numbers

Equipment and resources
A flower pot, card, scissors, black felt-tipped pen, red crayons.

Activity
Talk about ladybirds with the children and make sure that they all know what they look like, how small they are and where they can be found. Then suggest making some for a game. Cut small ovals from card, draw a black dividing line down the centre of each oval and colour one tip of each oval black. Draw black spots on both sides of the centre lines. Invite children to colour the ladybirds' bodies with the red crayons.

To play the game, spread the ladybirds out beside the upturned flower pot and count them together. Ask the children to close their eyes and hide some ladybirds under the flower pot while they are not looking. When they open their eyes again, ask them to count how many ladybirds are left.

Extension

Count the spots on the ladybirds instead of just counting each creature as one. Ask the children to work out how many ladybirds must be under the flower pot by counting how many are left and taking the number away from the original total.

Discussion

Introduce the idea of working out how many spots would be on three ladybirds if each had two spots. Support them while they think of ways to work out the answer and try them out. They could just count them all, if they were physically available, or they could count the correct one three times, or they could use their fingers or other aids to help.

Sorting into sets

Learning opportunities

* Exploring and describing colours, shapes, sizes and characteristics, similarities and differences
* Developing an understanding of the ways in which items can be linked to each other and grouped together according to their properties

Links to the Early Learning Goals

* Mathematics – Shape, space and measures

Also

* Understanding the world – The world

Equipment and resources

Building bricks and blocks of different colours, shapes, sizes and materials.

Activity

Work with three or four children. Put all the blocks together and try to decide on different categories that they might be sorted into. Ask the children to sort them into different colour sets, then to sort the coloured sets into big and small blocks or straight and curved blocks. When they are able to do this confidently, mix the blocks together again and suggest that they make a tower using just the yellow plastic blocks that have straight sides, or just the red wooden blocks that are not cubes.

Extension

Play a game of 'Find me….' Say, for example, 'Find me a block that is round and is plastic and is red.' Make the game appropriate to the individual abilities of the children. The more properties you state, the harder the task and the more concentration required.

Discussion

Talk about individual bricks and blocks and decide whether they have straight or curved edges, which are big and which small and what colours they are.

Big, bold butterflies

Learning opportunities
* Exploring and describing colours and two-dimensional shapes
* Recognizing patterns and characteristics of butterflies
* Using art and craft materials creatively

Links to the Early Learning Goals
* Mathematics – Shape, space and measures
Also
* Expressive arts and design – Exploring and using media and materials, Being imaginative
* Understanding the world – The world

Equipment and resources
Thick paint, paper, paintbrushes, scissors, pictures or photographs of butterflies.

Activity
Give the children pictures or photographs of butterflies to look at. Draw their attention to the colours and patterns on the butterflies' wings. Suggest to the children that you make a large display of bold butterflies in different colours. Give each child a large sheet of paper which has been folded down the middle. Let them choose what colour paint they would like. Invite them to choose some colours and to paint some shapes and patterns on one side of the fold. Then fold the paper in half and press. The child can open the sheet out to see the butterfly he has

made. When it is dry, you may cut the paper into a big
butterfly shape.

Group the butterflies by colour to display them, with a
written label for each colour set.

Extension

Make multi-coloured butterflies by the same method
and display them together.

Discussion

Count the number of butterflies in each set. Talk about
which butterflies are the boldest and which ones the
children think have the brightest colours.

Favourite colours

Learning opportunities
* Identifying different colours and understanding that people have different preferences and favourites
* Asking questions, making decisions and offering opinions

Links to the Early Learning Goals
* Understanding the world – People and communities

Also
* Communication and language – Speaking

Equipment and resources
Lots of different coloured blocks, counters and construction pieces.

Activity

Offer a mixture of coloured items to a small group of children. Tell them your favourite colour. Pick out a block or counter in that colour and say, for example, 'I like blue because it's the colour of the sky.' Invite the children to take turns to choose their favourite colour and encourage them to say why they like it.

Extension

Make a poster of the group's favourite colours.

Discussion

Ask the children to look carefully to see whether all the red things are the same shade of red. They will probably find more variation in blue and green than in red and yellow. Talk about which are the lightest and the darkest of the blue and green objects.

Making patterns

Learning opportunities
* Understanding and using simple computer programmes and games involving colours, shapes and patterns
* Recognizing and creating patterns using coloured objects

Links to the Early Learning Goals
* Understanding the world – Technology, The world

Also
* Mathematics – Shape, space and measures
* Expressive arts and design – Exploring and using media and materials

Equipment and resources
Computer and simple activity, game and drawing programmes suitable for pre-school aged children; different coloured counters, blocks or cotton reels.

Activity
Choose a suitable computer programme or game for the group of children and introduce it to them individually or in pairs. Demonstrate what the aim of the game or activity is, or the types of drawings or designs that can be made. Allow children time to practise using the mouse or keyboard and looking at the screen to see the effects of their actions. Activities may involve moving coloured pieces into places for patterns, by pressing arrow keys on a keyboard, or by clicking on them with a mouse and dragging them into position. Drawing programmes may allow

children to select colours and use them to make
designs by clicking on them and then moving the
mouse around the screen, or to select shapes with
arrow keys or a mouse and change their colours,
sizes and positions to create patterns and pictures. If
possible, connect the computer to a printer and help
children to print out some of their finished patterns to
display at the setting or to take home.

Use the counters, blocks or cotton reels to make a
line with a simple repeating colour pattern, such as:
yellow, blue, yellow, blue. Invite children to describe
and copy the pattern and then to create their own
patterns and describe and copy each other's.

Extension
Gradually introduce more complex repeating patterns.
For example, introduce three colours (yellow, blue,
red, yellow, blue, red), or include pairs (yellow, yellow,
blue, yellow, yellow, blue).

Discussion
Encourage children to secretly make up a pattern
and describe it verbally, so that a friend can try to
make it. When the friend has made their version,
the original pattern can be revealed to find out how
closely it matches. Talk with
the children about where
they see patterns in the world
around them. They may think
of clothes and furniture, shells
on a beach or snowflakes on a
window.

Spinning tops

Learning opportunities
* Observing the effects of movement on colours and the shades created as they mix
* Beginning to understand that the eye may be deceived by external influences
* Planning creative experiments with colours

Links to the Early Learning Goals
* Understanding the world – The world

Also

* Expressive arts and design – Exploring and using media and materials

Equipment and resources
Card; small saucers or circular lids; scissors; paint, crayons or coloured pencils or pens; small sharpened pencils.

Activity
Invite a small group of children to draw around the saucers or lids and cut out circles of card. Demonstrate how to divide each circle into halves, thirds or quarters and colour each section a different colour. When the children have coloured their circles, help them to push a small pencil carefully through the centre of each one to make tops. Encourage them to spin the tops and watch what happens to the colours.

Extension

Suggest that the children could colour the circles in different coloured rings, instead of sections, and find out whether they look different when spinning.

Discussion

Encourage the children to chat as they choose colours and designs for their tops. Ask them to predict what they think will happen when they spin them, then to say what they saw and whether they guessed correctly or were surprised.

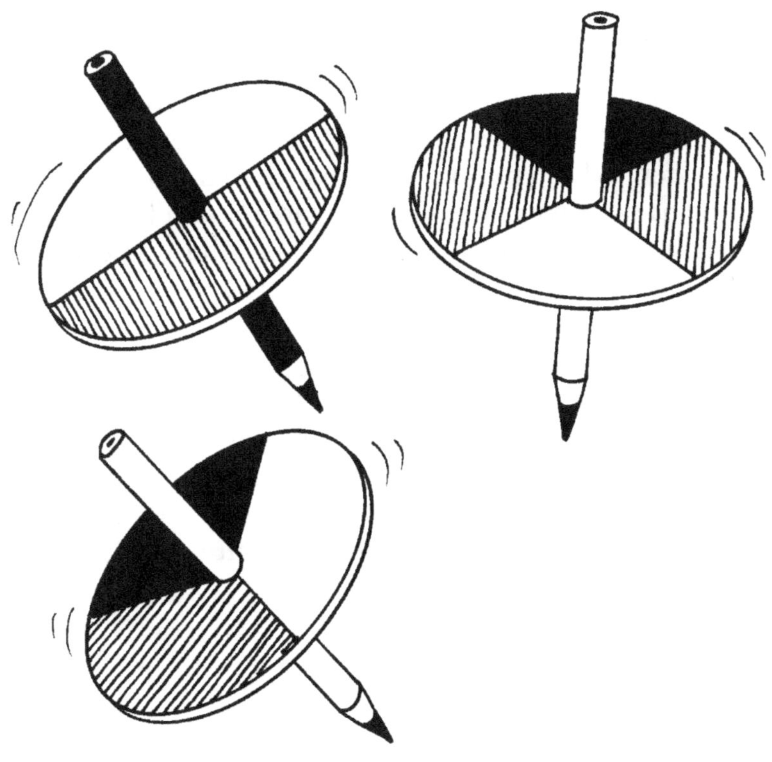

Make a rainbow

Learning opportunities

* Exploring the effect of one substance upon another and what happens when they are mixed together
* Developing an understanding of an event which occurs naturally in the outdoor environment

Links to the Early Learning Goals

* Understanding the world – The world

Equipment and resources

A washing-up bowl, water, vegetable oil, a sunny day.

Activity

Invite children to join you in the outdoor area on a sunny day. Prepare the equipment. Encourage children to help to pour the water into the bowl and then to pour some oil into the water. Stand the bowl in bright sunlight and, soon, everyone will be able to see a rainbow floating on top of the water.

Extension

Teach the children to sing the song 'Sing A Rainbow' for fun, but also tell them that some of the colours have been changed to make them easier and to make them rhyme. Help them to learn the real colours of the rainbow: red, orange, yellow, green, blue, indigo and violet.

Discussion

Ask children how they think that a rainbow gets into the water and whether it is the same as the one that appears in the sky. Talk about what they think it is that makes the rainbow appear and which colours they can see most easily.

Tell stories that try to explain rainbows, such as the story of Noah's Ark, in which the rainbow is said to be the sign of God's promise that the floods will never come again. According to an Incan (South American) legend, Rainbow was a beautiful young girl with magical powers. One day, when a huge monkey called Mancharu was chasing her, she managed to escape by turning herself into a ball of wool. Since then she has never dared to turn herself back into a girl. On rainy days you can see her making an arc in the sky as she jumps from river to river.

Colour walk

Learning opportunities
* Exploring the local environment to find a variety of items in a particular colour
* Observation, thinking and memory skills

Links to the Early Learning Goals
* Understanding the world – The world
Also
* Physical development – Moving and handling

Equipment and resources
A bag to collect things in, a camera.

Activity
Ask the group of children to choose which colour they would like to look for while out for a walk. Suggest to them that it may be easiest for the first walk to be looking for brown or green, as there are lots of outdoor things in those colours. When they have been on a few 'colour walks', they may like to choose a much rarer colour as a challenge. Explain to them that on your walk you are going to look for everything you can see in that colour and collect anything that's collectable. Take pictures of interesting things that can't be collected. For example, you could find brown leaves, shells and stones and take photographs of brown birds, tree trunks and fences. Talk through the walk afterwards, encouraging the children to remember everything they saw.

Extension

Involve the children in walks focusing on many different colours. Ask them to draw or paint something they saw on each walk when they return. Repeat some of the walks in different seasons and compare the colours.

Discussion

Talk with the children about the things they liked best and why they liked them. Ask them to remember whether they saw anything that was living, such as an insect, bird or animal. Remind them that plants and trees are also living things. Decide with the children which colour walk was the most exciting or interesting.

What happens?

Learning opportunities
* Exploring and experimenting with mixes and changes of colour, using acetates

Links to the Early Learning Goals
* Understanding the world – The world

Equipment and resources
Sheets of acetate in different colours, a variety of coloured objects or toys.

Activity
Invite small groups of children to set out objects and toys and to look at them through sheets of acetate in different colours. Discuss with them the ways in which things look different through red or green or other colours. Ask children to look at items around the room or garden and at their friends and to see how different they appear.

Extension
Help and support children if they would like to make coloured acetate glasses in their favourite colours. They could wear them while walking outside and see how many differences they notice.

Discussion

Ask the children to remember what colours the objects and toys really are before they look again without the acetate colours. Invite them to say which sheet they most like to look through and why.

Flower power

Learning opportunities
* Exploring and experimenting with plants, their need for water and their ability to take in colour
* Developing patience and an understanding that the results of some experiments are ongoing or cannot be observed immediately

Links to the Early Learning Goals
* Understanding the world – The world

Also

* Personal, social and emotional development – Managing feelings and behaviour

Equipment and resources
Jar or jug of water, three or four flowers (eg daffodils, cow parsley or carnations), some food colouring of a different colour.

Activity
Put the water in the jar and stir in several drops of food colouring. Cut the stems of your flowers at an angle and put the flowers in the jar. Wait for a few days to observe what happens to the flowers. Involve the children and invite them to participate actively in the processes throughout the experiment.

Extension

Try this experiment with other plants. Try leaving celery stalks in water with red food dye. Encourage children to paint 'before' and 'after' pictures of the flowers and plants or to draw diagrams of their experiments.

Discussion

Ask children to think about why the flowers have changed colour. Explain how the water rises from the bottom of the stems to the top and passes into the flowers to keep them alive, and how the food colouring is a liquid and so it mixes with the water.

Wax resist pictures

Learning opportunities

* Exploring and experimenting with a new art technique
* Discovering the effects of different craft materials when they are mixed together

Links to the Early Learning Goals

* Expressive arts and design – Exploring and using media and materials

Also

* Physical development – Moving and handling

Equipment and resources

Paper, thick wax crayons, paint (mixed to a very watery consistency).

Activity

Invite children to draw a picture or a pattern, using different coloured wax crayons. Remind them to press down firmly as they draw the lines. Support them if they wish to write their names in their favourite colours. When the pictures are finished, help the children to brush over them with the wet paint and leave them to dry.

Extension

Suggest that the children try to create a snowy picture using white wax crayons or candles and a dark blue paint for a winter night sky.

Discussion

Ask children if they know why the paint hasn't
covered the pictures and why they can still see their
wax drawings. Ask whether they think this technique
would work if you used pencils or felt-tipped pens
instead of wax crayons.

Colour mixing

Learning opportunities

* Exploring what happens when colours are mixed together
* Developing an awareness of primary and secondary colours and the effects of adding black and white

Links to the Early Learning Goals

* Expressive arts and design – Exploring and using media and materials, Being imaginative

Equipment and resources

Thick paper, paint brushes, red, blue and yellow paint.

Activity

Working with a small group of children, ask them to paint something in each of the three primary colours. Then put a small amount of two of the colours onto a clean sheet of paper and ask the children to mix them together. Watch and listen as they find out what colours they make and learn whether they are surprised. Continue until they have experimented with mixing:

* red and blue,
* red and yellow
* yellow and blue.

Extension

Try adding a drop at a time of black paint to each primary colour and secondary colour to see what happens. Do the same with white paint and watch what happens.

Discussion

Invite children to show their painted colour charts to the group and to explain their experiments and their results.

Printing colours

Learning opportunities

* Exploring and experimenting with the technique of printing, using different materials
* Discovering which methods and materials are more effective than other
* Creating patterns with repeating colours and designs
* Improving control and coordination of small movements

Links to the Early Learning Goals

* Expressive arts and design – Exploring and using media and materials, Being imaginative

Also

* Mathematics – Shape, space and measures
* Physical development – Moving and handling

Equipment and resources

Powder paints in several colours (mixed to a thick consistency); a variety of objects to print with (stickle bricks, lego, cotton reels, sponges, corks, potatoes, etc.); water pots; paintbrushes; different types and colours of paper and card.

Activity

Work with three or four children at a time. Invite them to choose objects, colours and papers. Demonstrate how to use paintbrushes to put enough paint onto the printing objects and then press the objects onto the paper again and again, until there is no paint left on them. Explain how to wash the brushes in the water pots. Encourage the children to choose different colours to paint onto different objects and print onto the paper or card.

Extension
Encourage the children to make up patterns of repeating colours and shapes with their printing objects, or to make a picture.

Discussion
Talk with the children about their experiments and what they have learned. For example, does how much paint you put onto the printing object make a difference to its effectiveness and does pressing down firmly make a better print than banging the object down? Ask the children how many prints they managed to make each time they painted an object, or whether the number varied with different colours and objects. Discuss the different objects and ask which were the best for printing.

Colour collage

Learning opportunities
* Exploring the colours and textures of different materials, both natural and man-made
* Grouping colours together and recognizing that there may be many different shades of one colour (particularly of colours such as blue, green and brown)

Links to the Early Learning Goals
* Expressive arts and design – Exploring and using media and materials

Also
* Understanding the world – The world

Equipment and resources
A large collection of assorted pieces suitable for use in collage work – including such materials as fabric, plastic, paper, buttons, flower petals, card, tissue paper, wool, thread, string, leaves, twigs, etc; laminator; sticky labels; glue; sticky tape.
Also: encourage children to collect their own natural materials from the outdoor area and craft and recycled pieces from inside the setting, to use in their collages.

Activity
Invite a small group of children to create colour collages. Encourage them each to choose a colour and to sort through the materials available and collect the pieces of that colour that they would like to use. Ask them to arrange the pieces on a sheet of paper or card and to attach them lightly with glue or sticky

tape to keep them in position. Laminate the sheets to make the collages. Support children as they write their names and the colours they have chosen onto sticky labels and attach them to their collages.

Extension

Make 'feelie' collages to go with the colour collages. Stick the textured materials to pieces of card with glue, but don't laminate them. Display all the work together.

Discussion

Ask if they can identify the lightest and the darkest coloured objects in the collages and count how many different shades there are.

Tissue test

Learning opportunities

* Experimenting with making creative patterns using coloured tissue papers
* Exploring the effects of light on colours and materials
* Control and coordination in small movements and particularly cutting skills

Links to the Early Learning Goals

* Expressive arts and design – Exploring and using media and materials, Being imaginative

Also

* Physical development – Moving and handling

Equipment and resources

Large pieces of card, a quantity of tissue paper in a variety of colours, glue, scissors.

Activity

Offer children the pieces of card and scissors and invite them to cut out holes of different shapes and sizes. (Demonstrate how to fold the card lightly and make a snip, then open it out and cut outwards from the small hole. If children cut in from the sides, they will not be able to make enclosed holes and the activity will not work.) Provide a variety of coloured tissue paper pieces and ask the children to cut or tear the colours and sizes that they need and to put them over the holes they have made. They will need to spread glue around the edges of the holes on the back

of the sheet and stick on coloured pieces of tissue that
are slightly bigger all around.

Encourage the children to experiment with different
numbers of layers and different colours. They could
have some holes covered with just a single layer of
tissue, some with more than one layer of the same
colour and some with different coloured tissues
layered over each other. Show the children how
to hold the pieces of card up to the light to see the
results.

Extension
Make 'stained glass windows' using this technique
and display them on the windows if possible.

Discussion
Talk with the children about what happens to the
colours when the light shines through them, which
are the brightest colours, what new colours are made
by mixing two or more layers and why they think
the colours become more 'smudgy' when they are
overlapped.

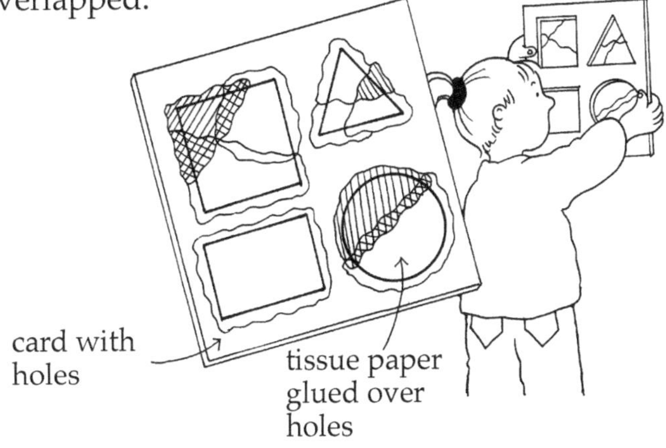